Bromley Libraries
30128 80316 512 8

How to Be

RESPONSIBLE

A Question and Answer Book About Responsibility

by Emily James

a Capstone company — publishers for children

Responsibility is a big word. But we all show responsibility every day.

Being responsible means doing the things you are supposed to do.

Sometimes being responsible means doing things you don't want to do.

There are lots of ways to show you are responsible.

Carter and his brother have broken a lamp while playing. His brother wants to lie about what happened.

What should Carter do to show he's responsible?

Carter tells his mum the truth. Being truthful shows responsibility.

Have you ever had to choose between telling the truth and lying?

Lily's bedroom is a mess!

What should Lily do to show she's responsible?

Lily cleans her room without being asked. Tidying up after yourself shows responsibility.

Do you keep your room clean?

Gunner has a dentist appointment.

What should Gunner do to show responsibility?

Gunner and his dad make sure they get to the dentist's on time. Arriving on time is part of being responsible.

What can you do to make sure you arrive on time for appointments?

Sofia has got a new puppy.

What should Sofia do to show she's responsible?

Sofia feeds and walks her puppy every day. Taking care of your pets shows responsibility.

In what other ways can you take care of a pet?

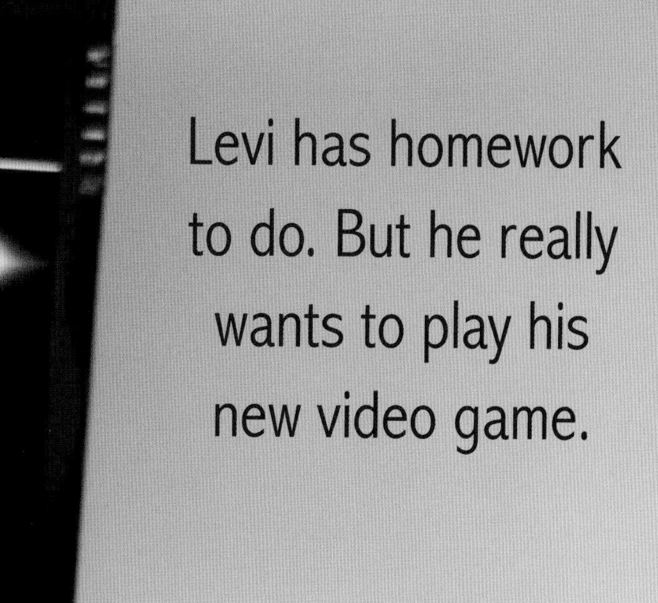

Levi has homework to do. But he really wants to play his new video game.

What should Levi do to show responsibility?

Levi does his homework.
Finishing your homework
first shows responsibility.

Do you do your homework before playing?

Emma's sister asks if she can have a biscuit. It's against the rules to have snacks before dinner.

What should Emma do to show she's responsible?

Emma tells her sister she can't have a biscuit. Following the rules shows responsibility.

Has anyone ever asked you to break the rules?

What did you do?

Kate didn't revise
for her maths test.
She did poorly in the test.

What can she do to show responsibility?

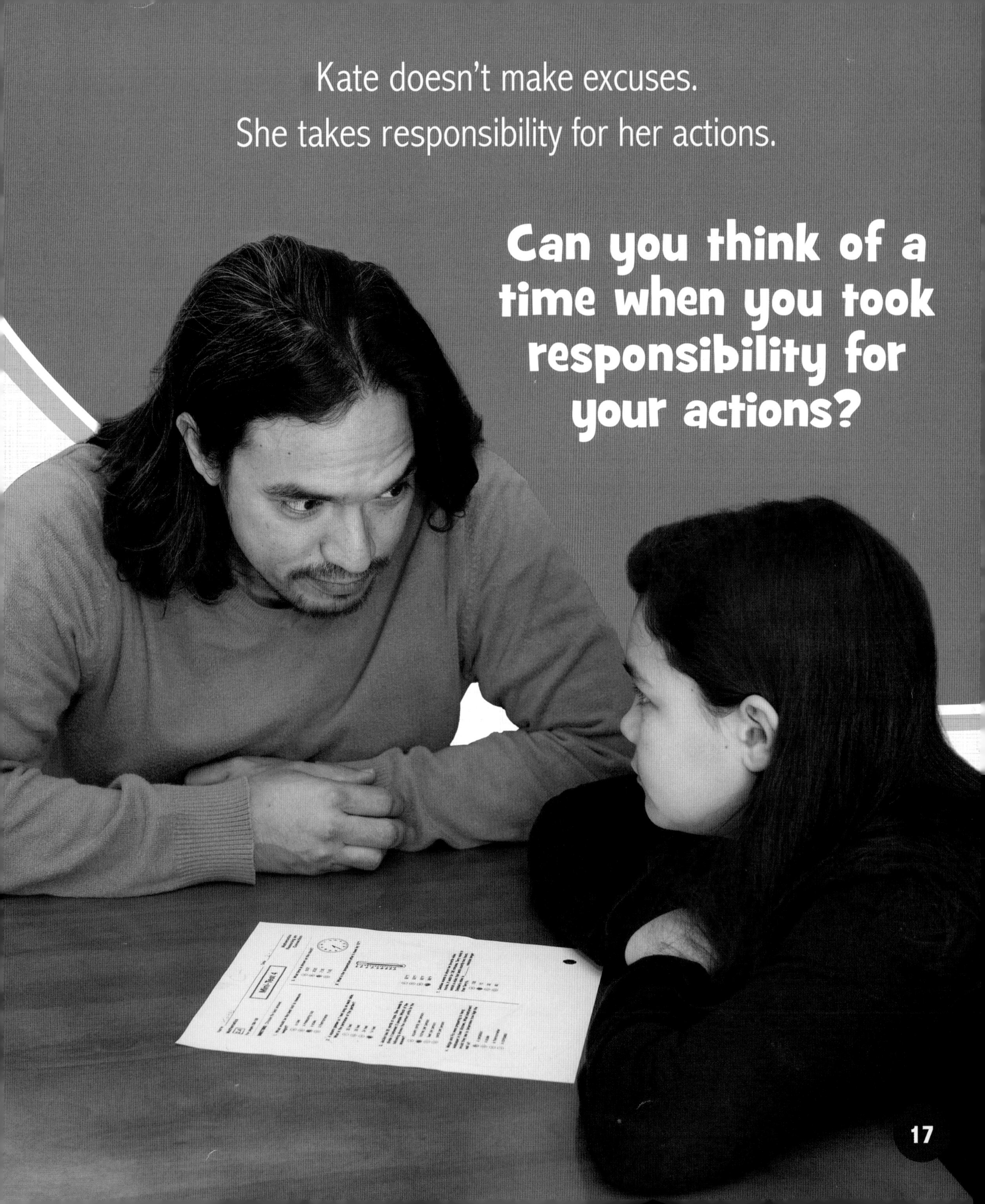

Kate doesn't make excuses.
She takes responsibility for her actions.

Can you think of a time when you took responsibility for your actions?

Colin promises to help

with the housework.

What can Colin do to show he's responsible?

Colin washes the dishes after dinner. Keeping a promise shows responsibility. What promises have you made?

Have you ever broken a promise? How did it make you feel?

Julia knows it's important to take care of the environment.

What should she do to show responsibility?

Julia recycles her water bottle. Doing your part to help the environment shows responsibility.

What do you do to protect the environment?

Eli is getting ready for bed.

What should Eli do to show he's responsible?

Eli brushes his teeth without being asked. Looking after your teeth shows responsibility.

How do you look after your teeth?

Olivia's library book is due back today.

What should Olivia do to show she's responsible?

Olivia returns her library book.
Returning the things you
borrow shows responsibility.
Can you think of something you've borrowed?

Did you return it when you were supposed to?

Mia and Logan are partners
for a science project.

**What should they do
to show responsibility?**

Mia and Logan split the work.
Doing your part shows you are responsible.

Have you ever had to share work with someone?

James is excited about going outside after lunch. He accidentally bumps the table and spills his drink.

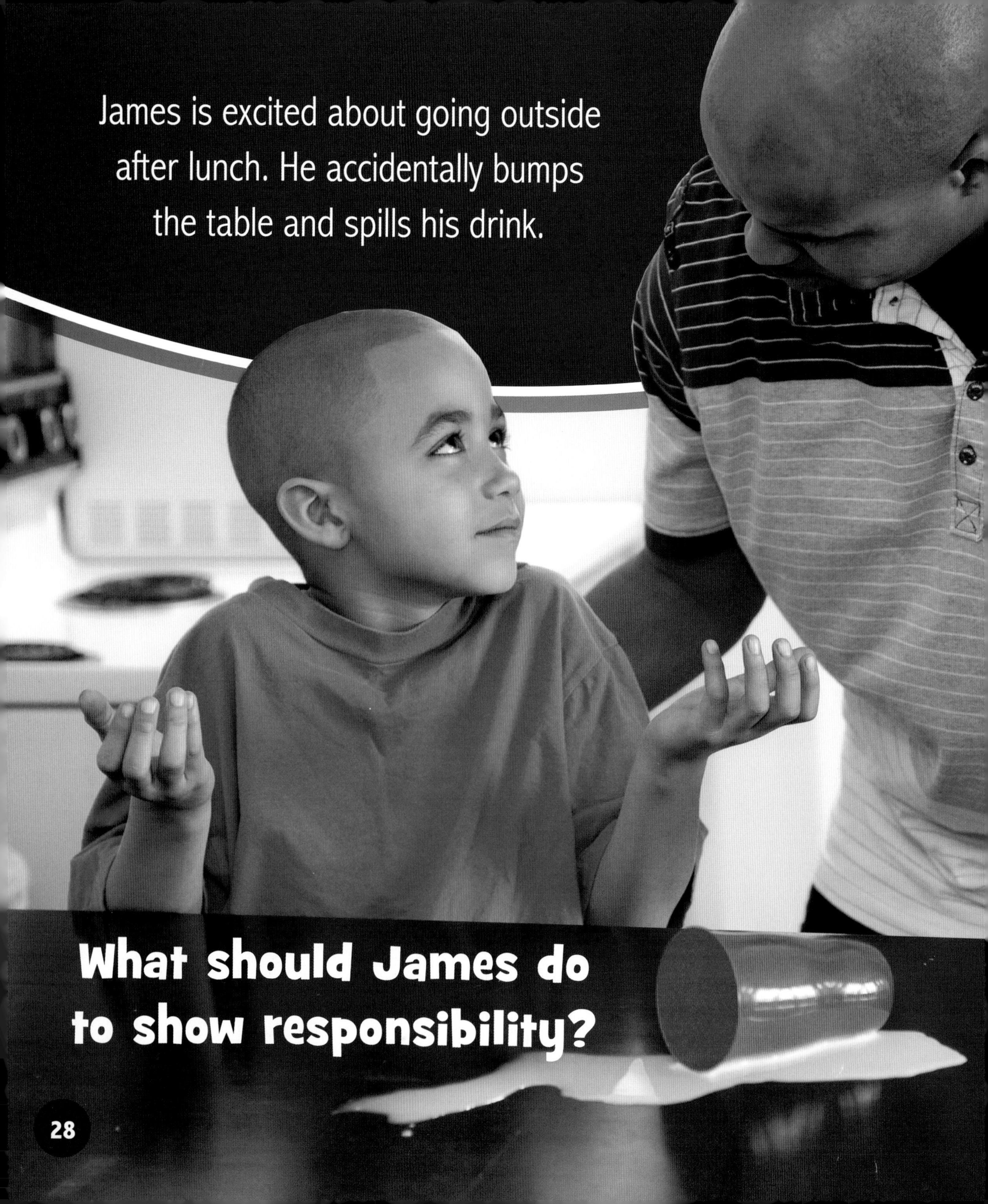

What should James do to show responsibility?

James stays inside and cleans up the mess.
Even though the spill was an accident,
it's his responsibility to clean it up.

Have you ever had to miss out on something fun because you were being responsible?

Glossary

accidentally without meaning to

environment all of the trees, plants, water and soil

excuse a reason you give to explain a mistake or why you have done something wrong

housework jobs that need to be done around the home; washing dishes and taking out the rubbish are housework

partner a person who works or does some other activity with another person

responsible doing what you say you will do; people who are responsible keep promises and follow rules

Comprehension questions

1. How does Julia show responsibility towards the environment?
2. Making excuses does not show responsibility. What is an excuse? Hint: Use your glossary!
3. Can you think of a time you were responsible? What did you do?

Find out more

Books

How Should I Behave?, Mick Manning and Brita Granstrom (Franklin Watts, 2017)

I Can Help (My Behaviour), Liz Lennon (Franklin Watts, 2015)

What Does it Mean to be British?, Nick Hunter (Raintree, 2017)

Websites

bbc.co.uk/education/topics/zw339j6/resources/1
Find lots of videos showing how you can be responsible in many different ways.

bbc.co.uk/education/clips/z8587hv
Watch a video to show how you can help care for the environment.

Index

Raintree is an imprint of Capstone Global Library Limited, a company incorporated in England and Wales having its registered office at 264 Banbury Road, Oxford, OX2 7DY – Registered company number: 6695582

www.raintree.co.uk
myorders@raintree.co.uk

ISBN 978 1 4747 4387 7
21 20 19 18 17
10 9 8 7 6 5 4 3 2 1

British Library Cataloguing in Publication Data
A full catalogue record for this book is available from the British Library.

Acknowledgements
All photographs by Capstone Studio/Karon Dubke, except:
Shutterstock: michaeljung, 26, 27, RoyStudioEU throughout, (background texture)

Editorial Credits
Jaclyn Jaycox, editor; Heidi Thompson, designer; Jo Miller, media researcher;
Laura Manthe, production specialist; Marcy Morin, scheduler
Every effort has been made to contact copyright holders of material reproduced in this book. Any omissions will be rectified in subsequent printings if notice is given to the publisher.

Printed and bound in China.